Dear Deanna,
   May you always
know the "Faithful
Hope" of Jesus!
         Love,
      Fae

Faithful Hope

Faithful Hope

A 40 Day Devotional for Hurting People

All scripture quotations, unless otherwise indicated, are taken from the Holy Bible, New International Version®, NIV®. Copyright ©1973, 1978, 1984 by Biblica, Inc.™ Used by permission of Zondervan. All rights reserved worldwide.

www.zondervan.com

Publisher: Fae Dunn

fdunnbook@gmail.com

ISBN-978-0-9882407-2-8

This book is dedicated to those who need hope.

It is intended to bring glory to God!

For without Him, I could not have

written one word.

The Lure of Chocolate

He touched my heart when he looked at me and I was vulnerable, needing affirmation. I had a deep desire within me for what only he could provide. The satisfaction of approval, acceptance and yes, even love—at least for the moment.

He seduced me with his kindness and the persistence that was always there. He was everywhere I turned, forever staring at me. I resisted. Still he seemed to be drawing me ever closer, my heart being drawn to him.

He touched me and I felt his warmth, as if his beating heart needed me as much as I needed him. This is where I started to break down, to give in to my desire. Taking my eyes ever so briefly off of my Lord, I began playing with the idea in my mind. What if I, just this one time, partook of the forbidden fruit? Certainly God had provided Chocolate for my pleasure.

I was losing my grip on the One who mattered most, instead I was being influenced by the words that seemed to make it acceptable. I paused to question what was so wrong with just one time, or perhaps two? To taste Chocolate, ever so smooth, so sweet to my lips, just a small bite of Chocolate, I would savor its taste. Yes, certainly God had provided!

I gave in, once again, to the lure of Chocolate but found it to be a painful and bitter ending. Isn't that the way it is with sin?

In itself, Chocolate is not wrong or bad in any way but

when you look at it as a weapon, being used to take you down the wrong path, it can be very dangerous. What is the lure in your life? For me it is Chocolate, for I am sensitive to this delectable treat, causing me terrible migraines and depression. Thus, every so often, I justify my actions and allow myself to be lured just one more time. Truly, there is nothing wrong with Chocolate but when we partake of the fruit that we know will cause pain and perhaps death in the end, it is an altogether different story.

One person's forbidden fruit can be an acceptable, wonderful treat for another. And so it is with sin. For me, it is Chocolate...dark and sweet...calling me. I struggle! For another it may be sensuality. For yet another it may be alcohol or drugs. We each have our own personal sin that we wrestle with. We need to be so careful, to not look at another person and think their struggle is nothing...for it is their personal struggle...theirs to endure.

It's not the temptation that is sinful, it is when we give in to that temptation. I've given in to temptation a number of times and yet, His grace envelopes me. He's always there to forgive me when I humble myself in true confession of my sin. So together, let's experience His faithful hope.

My Dear Readers,

Many years ago, a dear friend, Pat, challenged our Sunday School group to read through the Bible. Whether it took us a year or five years, she wanted us to experience all the benefits that come from reading the Bible from cover to cover. She also suggested that we get a version of the Bible that we understand. That challenge has taken me on an adventure, an adventure of longing for God's Word daily! I have continued daily Bible reading for over 30 years now, being challenged to live my life as God has called me.

Therefore, I am excited for you! This book is meant to be that same challenge for you. This book is intended to be used in whatever way that meets your needs. A daily devotional. A Bible study. A help for new Christians. A revival tool. Whether you are looking to start a relationship with Jesus, the Christ; or you want to strengthen that relationship. May this book be a means to bring each of us to a right relationship with God the Father, through His Word. He is the only One who can help us through the hard times as well as the good times.

What follows is God's gift to help me grow and I wanted to share it with you. As you read this, may the glory be given to Him as He calls each of us to a closer walk with Him. Though I do not know you, He does. He knows what each of us needs at this very moment and He has drawn you to this book for a purpose.

Perhaps you will want to start a separate notebook and journal each of your 40 days. By doing this, you will be able to look back upon this journey to see your progress. I know in the future there will be times of discouragement where this journal will be of great support, helping you see the progress you've made along the way, whether large or small.

Or perhaps, you will just want to read through and challenge yourself each of the 40 days. Maybe you are skeptical of this whole God thing. I pray that you see Jesus throughout the book and come to know Him personally. This book is a tool to help you along the path, but the Bible is your main guide to what is living and true! There is nothing else quite like the Word of God to start each day. I have chosen to capitalize pronouns pertaining to the Lord, it is my way of showing respect to Him.

My life has not been always easy, but let me tell you that it is through the pain and hardships of life that I've grown the most. It is through the heartache that I have experienced the Refiner's Fire and come out stronger because of it. But the times that I've been happy and content have been the hardest times to keep my eyes on Jesus. Yet He's always there, in every situation of life.

So, perhaps you are asking yourself "why would I want to read a book that draws me closer to the Lord? Everything is going well! In fact, I don't have financial problems, health problems, or relationship problems...life is very good!" But, may I ask, do you still have an empty spot within your soul, a longing for something more, something deeper? Or do you long for peace and joy that just doesn't ever seem to satisfy your soul? Well, tie your hat on because you are about

4

to take a ride into the Jesus Zone! Enter with caution! Enter with reverence! Enter knowing that God is about to do a work in you! And you will be better in the end.

In no way is this devotional meant to bring condemnation upon you, quite the opposite. God has used the many illustrations in my own life to bring me to conviction and repentance. I once heard it said that conviction brings life because we are pointed to Jesus, while, on the other hand, condemnation brings death because it makes you think you have no hope.

In my excitement for you, I want you to know that these words are as much for me as they are for you. He has called me to write but I am not perfect by any means for I am right there by your side, crying my eyes out or jumping for joy, stretching my spiritual walk each step I take. Won't you take my hand and let us walk together? For God has promised that He is with us, as we join together with one another to bring glory to Him.

In His Love and Service,

Fae

Personal challenges:

Day 1

How Firm Is Your Foundation?

Firm: Solid, Sturdy, Stable, Safe
Scripture reading: Luke 6: 46-49; Rev 1:3

The foundation of any building must be structurally sound. It is on this foundation that the rest of the building will find support. Without a strong, firm foundation the structure above cannot stand.

Do you grasp the principle Jesus was trying to teach from the scripture reading? Jesus points out that if we hear what He is telling us but do not make it relevant in our everyday lives, our foundation is flawed. What are you building your life upon? The man/woman in your life? Your children? Your job? How big or small your house is? Your bank account?   Will this type of a foundation be strong enough to go through the storms of this life?

How are we supposed to know what God wants us to do? This question is all too familiar to so many and yet, the answer is right at hand. Anything worthwhile must take effort on our part, in fact, it is hard work. It is well worth the endeavor as we are determined to find out what He wants for our lives.

God promises us that those who read God Word will be blessed and as we conform to God's Word, we will be blessed beyond measure. Revelation 1:3 exhorts us to take what we hear, read and comprehend it and obey it. Simply put, it means to read it and then do it. This simple statement is calling us to move out of our comfort zone, being obedient to what God is calling us to do.

So as we start on this 40 day journey with our Lord, it will involve spending time in the Word of God daily. Some of you may already use a program for reading the Bible but others may be brand new at this whole relational thing with our Lord. I use Bible Pathway Ministries (see Appendix A) to help me get through the Bible each year. Others use a chronological Bible or a suggested reading in their Bible. Whatever you use, you will find it helpful to read a version of the Bible that you can totally understand. Remember during times of stress, pain and hardship, it is harder for us to comprehend so get a version that will minister to you.

One thing I can guarantee, your foundation will gradually grow stronger day by day as you get into the Word of God, the Holy Bible, and ask God to show you what He wants you to learn that day only. Let Him be your teacher. Be a willing student who wants to strengthen your foundation.

The most amazing part of this journey (to me) is no matter how many times we read the Bible, God will show you something new, something relevant to what is happening in your life at that very moment.

Journaling: Write a couple of paragraphs honestly describing your foundation at this time. Is it solid? Is it safe? See if your description is much like our vocabulary words or quite the opposite. Be honest! This is for your eyes only. Also, write down what version of the Bible you are using so that in the future, you will come to know if that is the right one for you. Do you know Jesus? What is that relationship like?

Prayer: Our Precious Heavenly Father, may You touch my heart this day so I may have a longing to know You more. Give me a willing desire to build that sturdy foundation that only comes from You. In Jesus Name…Amen

Personal Challenges:

Day 2

Perseverance

Persevere: continue, persist, to carry on
Scripture reading: Matthew 6:25-34

What is God teaching you today? I seem to be a slow learner much of the time. Just about the time I think I've learned a lesson; I am reminded that I had already learned that lesson once before. Or was it twice? Well anyway, I have to learn the same lesson all over again. Do you ever do that? I must ask Him over and over again to give me a heart that will persevere through the lessons of life.

We worry about our job or lack of a job, we worry about how we are going to pay the bills, we worry about our car, we worry about our kids or grandkids. The list is endless. You make your own list, I have mine. How many times have we seen God answer our prayers and yet, we forget and worry once more? As He is teaching us to not worry, He is also teaching us a much bigger lesson of life and that is learning to carry on through the bad times as well as the good.

So, let us persevere through those times of worry, let us be reminded that we are worth far more to our Heavenly Father than anything we can comprehend. The day will come when we can say with all honesty, "consider it all joy, my brothers, whenever you face trials of many kinds, because you know that the testing of your faith develops perseverance." (James 1:2-3)

And so, perseverance continues to be a progression as we walk hand in hand with Jesus. It is not always easy but He is always there. James 1:4 gives us hope in this walk with perseverance because it promises that we will "be mature and complete, not lacking anything". I don't know about you, but I look forward to that day!

What a privilege it is to be loved so much by our Lord that He trusts us enough to allow those trials. This is amazing to me. As we persevere He is maturing us...being fully developed and complete. Isn't that awesome that God would love each of us so deeply as to allow us to go through trials? Are you ready to persevere to the point of not lacking anything?

I do not always have a good attitude as I face a trial. My attitude often gets worse when I am in the middle of a trial. But God gently reminds me at some point (when I am ready to listen) that I can count on Him to get me through the trial. I have learned that I need to ask for wisdom and it is there when I ask! But I have to humble myself enough to ask, to realize that I have a need for God's precious, perfect wisdom.

Yes indeed, in all circumstances, the trials are there to mature us to His blessed hope and unfailing love. Let me encourage you that God loves and trusts you enough to allow those trials and to bring you to a new level of Himself. Through perseverance, we will learn to humble ourselves and look to Him. He is waiting with open arms.

Journaling: Do you worry? Can you see that as you persevere, and mature in Him, you will not worry as much? What memory verse will you start working on today to help you worry less and to persevere through those trials?

Prayer: Dear Lord, I fall short so often. I am thankful that You trust me with each trial. Help me Lord, not to worry so much; to be able to give it to You. Give me the wisdom to see that each little worry is a time that I can trust You more. In Jesus Name…Amen

Personal Challenges:

Day 3

The Will of the Father

Will: determination, motivation, strength of character

Scripture Reference: Romans 7:14-20; Ephesians 4:20-24

Have you ever thought about our habits, behaviors and words being a visible reflection of our attitude? Our attitude is made up of our inner, unseen beliefs, convictions and opinions and it is our attitude that motivates us. The character of a person is seen by what they do and what they say. Years ago I heard a sermon that helped me better understand where my character comes from. This insight helped me to stop and ponder if my attitude could, in the least bit, reflect the will of the Father. It further brought a lot of questions to my mind.

Do I willingly sin and often justify my behavior? If God sees sin as rebellion, then am I rebelling against the One who I want to please? Furthermore, am I living in this state of sin by justifying it? Has my heart become so hard? Although these are hard questions and seem to be something we might not want to confront, we each must face ourselves truthfully in order to grow to the point of wanting to do the will of the Father.

We see it every day, in those around us and in ourselves. We justify the small stuff not realizing it leads us to the bigger. I struggle with eating...I justify why I should be allowed to eat that donut. It has taken me years to realize that God isn't trying to punish me by not letting me eat certain foods (I have many food allergies). He is actually trying to teach me to change my attitude, what really motivates me. He wants me to look to the Word of God when I have struggles (yes, even with food) and not justify my sinful behavior.

Yes, as we bathe ourselves in the Word of God, He constantly reminds us with the truth of His Word. If we do not feel the gentle nudging of the Holy Spirit (OK, sometimes He does have to shout), then perhaps you need to check your heart. God is so faithful, He willingly wants to walk along side us right now, each and every day, for the rest of our lives.

Journaling: Write down one area in your life where you are struggling? Then take another look at that struggle, is it just the surface or does God have something much deeper He is trying to show you? Make a note of this and write down what your attitude is right now. Can you see some small area where you will need to change your attitude to match the will of the Father's?

Prayer: Father God, help me with my attitude. Help me not to justify my sinful behavior and to be willing to do Your will. Thank you Lord for showing me this area and giving me Your insight to change. In Jesus Name...Amen

Personal Challenges:

Day 4

Anticipating God's Best

Anticipate: expect, await, to be hopeful of

Scripture reading: Genesis 39:21-23

Do you think when Joseph's brothers sold him into slavery he was anticipating God's best for his life? Certainly this act of mercy was better than death (their original plan) but it was not exactly the fulfillment of Joseph's dreams, of his brothers bowing down to him. Genesis 37 says several times that Joseph's brothers hated him and were jealous of him. God, in His great wisdom, knew Joseph needed some refining before He could use him.

Have you ever noticed that God has to do some major refining in each of our lives before we learn the lesson He is trying to teach us? I have.

Let's continue to look at Joseph's life. He landed a pretty decent job once he arrived in Egypt. Genesis 39 says that "the Lord was with Joseph and he prospered" (v 2) and "the Lord gave him success in everything he did" (v 3). On top of all that, he "was well-built and handsome" (v 6b). WOW! He seemed to have it all. That is, until Potiphar's wife noticed him.

Even though Joseph did the right thing and chose not to "sin against God" (v 9), as he fled from her, "he left his cloak in her hand" (v 12) and she lied to the servants and her husband about what had happened. Joseph's master "burned with anger" (v 19) and he put

Joseph in prison. Yet, in verse 21, we read that "the Lord was with him; he showed him kindness and granted him favor in the eyes of the prison warden".

Joseph never gave up on doing his best for God. He never let bitterness take root in his heart. He moved forward by interpreting the dreams of two prisoners who came from Pharaoh's house (Gen 40:8-23). Yet, it would be a couple more years before the chief cupbearer would remember what Joseph had done for him and tell Pharaoh about Joseph's ability to interpret dreams.

As the story of Joseph unfolds, years are passing! Not hours or days or even weeks but YEARS. This is a hard lesson for us to learn in our microwave society. Often we expect God to answer our prayers within our time frame. We can be impulsive, making abrupt and hasty choices. Or we can be impatient. But the Good News is, no matter what you are experiencing this very day, God has a purpose and His timing is perfect.

Journaling: Have you ever looked at the happenings in your life as being directed by God? Afterwards, could you then understand why you had to go through that incident? Are you experiencing anything right now that you have wondered why it is happening?

Prayer: Heavenly Father, I thank you for Your great wisdom in directing my life and teaching me along the way. Help me Lord, to be more aware of your presence. In Jesus Name…Amen

Personal Challenges:

Day 5
The Boundaries of Reconciliation

Boundary: limit, constraint, regulate, check

Scripture reading: Gen 42:6-24

I would like to continue looking at Joseph's life. Here in the United States we talk a lot about freedom. It is exciting to see the freedom that Joseph experienced as a leader in Egypt and a follower of the One True God. He also set his brothers free in a way they never expected.

Joseph had the surprise of his life when he found his brothers before him, bowing down, just as he had dreamed many years earlier. He had experienced mistreatment at the hand of these men who were now asking for food.

It is obvious that Joseph forgave his brothers, for he did not have them killed on the spot. But he also did not trust them. By putting them in jail for a couple of days, he allowed himself time to develop a strategy on how to evaluate their sincerity. I believe he wanted to test their character, to see if they were genuine, to determine if they had changed and were truly repentant of their sin. Were they honest and reliable or were they the same scoundrels?

When Joseph had his brothers released from jail, he set some pretty powerful boundaries "...do this and you will live..." (Gen 42:18) He did not dwell on what they had done years ago; he wanted to know what kind of men they had become. Would he see a change in each of his brothers? Were they now more concerned about family members?

Years ago, neither Joseph's cries for mercy (as a teen) nor their father's tears brought the repentance needed from these men. As Joseph presented different challenges into his brothers' lives, he saw remorse and repentance. They were truly sorry for what they had done to him and to their father.

In our lives, we will experience times of remorseful repentance. In seeking God's will, we will be pierced in our heart and mind because of the sin we have committed. When those we have hurt see that we are sincere (through their own testing), they will know that we can be trusted. Our responsibility is to confess our sins, not only to God but to the offended person showing the remorse we are feeling. We strive for a finished work hoping reconciliation can take place.

Journaling: Reconciliation is hard, intentional work but it honors God. Has God brought someone to mind that you have hurt or sinned against? Are you ready to take steps of reconciliation? Remember, that person may set boundaries in the reconciliation process, so seek Christ's forgiving love as your first step. And remember, it is a process.

Prayer: Lord, I thank you for a change in my heart as I admit my sin, confessing it to You but also taking the responsibility of going to that person and telling them how sorry I am for my behavior towards them.

Help me Lord each step of the way to bring healing and reconciliation. In Jesus Name…Amen

Personal Challenges:

Day 6

His Grace

Grace: kindness, mercy, leniency

Scripture reading: James 1: 2-12; Romans 5:8

Learning to endure through times of testing is a process as we walk with Christ.

Often I think of all that Joseph went through when I am experiencing misery on my life journey. I am reminded that God knows what I need in order to get me to the place where He can use me. Joseph is my mentor as I walk this road of learning about God's grace.

Joseph was a dreamer and loved to share his dreams. The jealous half- brothers were used by God, without them knowing it, taking Joseph to a place where he would end up serving God and man to save an entire nation. A nation that extended help to those wicked half-brothers. Do you suppose that God was trying to teach them something too? Are we sometimes so stuck in our ways that we are going to do it our way, no matter what God wants?

Sure thing! I know we can all remember times when we were on the side of Joseph, being hurt, abused, and ridiculed by those around us and if we want to be really honest, we have also been on the other side as well. We have said a hurtful word (or two) to someone close to us, or we have acted hastily in making a decision that affected those we love or our behavior has been out and out immature and abusive. Yes, we all sin in some way that can cause another person to be crushed or hurt by us.

Just as God used the circumstances that Joseph went through to get him to the point of being a humble servant…making decisions for millions of people, God uses circumstances to soften us, to smooth rough edges, or to change our thinking. The Lord is always on time! He is there beside us, guiding us, teaching us (if we will only listen!). His ways, His desires for us, His grace, love and peace are there for us to take hold of. He longs for us to learn these lessons! I remember a time when I was struggling with a situation, I had a counselor say to me, "God must really love you because He's giving you extra grace to get through this." Extra grace! We all need that from time to time as we persevere through what He's trying to teach us.

Throughout Scripture, God uses circumstances and other people to get His chosen ones where He wants them. Have you ever felt like you were wandering in the desert? Have you ever felt like God has abandoned you? Have you ever said "I can't take it anymore"?

I think if I were in Joseph's many circumstances over the years, I would have wondered if God had forgotten me. Can you imagine? He didn't even have the Bible to read every day! Yet he prayed and knew that God was with him. Scripture tells us that "the Lord was with him" (Gen 39:3; 21; 23), just as He is with each of us throughout distressful times.

Are you going through troubles because of your own sin? Perhaps it is sin we do not want to even admit! But, let's be honest, God already knows! There are always consequences to our behavior. Often our pain is caused by our own poor choices but it is so much easier to blame someone else! God is asking us to take a hard look at ourselves. He wants us to acknowledge our sin, to confess it, to change our behavior and to start living for Him. His desire for our lives is to build Godly character! He does not want us to compromise our values; He wants us to be children of integrity, to be pure in heart, mind and spirit.

Joseph had a choice to make when he went through the trying times. You and I have a choice to make when going through the hard times. What a loving process.

Journaling: Take a few minutes to look at your life. What has God been trying to teach you? What have you learned from tough circumstances so far? Is He using people around you as an instrument? Have you accepted His grace today?

Prayer: Father God, although trials are difficult, I thank you for loving me so much and trusting me to handle those times of difficulty. I also thank you for your grace, love and mercy. Without You, I am helpless! In Jesus Name...Amen

Personal Challenges:

Day 7

Have you considered my servant?

Consider: think about, mull over, reflect on

Scripture reading: Esther 4; Job 1:6-12

Have you ever been prompted by the Holy Spirit? Perhaps you were prompted to give a compliment to someone who needed to hear your kind words. Or maybe it was a kind deed. Oftentimes, we are prompted to pray for someone dear to us and other times, it is prayers for someone we barely know.

Well, in the summer of 1995, I was prompted to write the words, "If I perish, I perish" (Esther 4:16b) on a small piece of paper and put it on my refrigerator. I had no idea what God had in mind in the months and years to follow! In Esther's case she said those words as she took the risk of losing her prestigious position as Queen, or even losing her life. I, on the other hand, had no prestigious position, but God has used my willingness to die to self, to rip from my very being those things which kept me from serving Him. But in order to use me, I had to take the same type of risk as Esther.

Isn't it just like our Lord to care enough for us to allow us to go through the pain and agony of defeat, of loss of health, of loss of family and friends, and loss of possessions? He is teaching us what is truly valuable. He provides and protects us as we respond to His promptings.

The sufferings, the shame, the guilt, the half-truths that are said are all testing our faith, just like Job. Unlike Job's friends (with friends like that, who need enemies?) Job gained spiritual insight. Just as it was in both Esther's and Job's life, it is today. I long for spiritual insight! Don't you? I accept His blessings with open arms. Don't you? Yet when He brings me through another fire, should I not be thankful for the afflictions as well? Should I not see His great love for me as He cleanses me? Should I not realize that through such difficulties my faith is growing ever so much stronger?

In moments of quietness, I actually do have an understanding of what He is doing in my life. But honestly, during those desperate, painful times I often cry out, "I can't take it Lord!" I long for the trial to pass and peace to come once again. There are times when I do not feel that I have a friend in this whole world. I long for someone to take me in their arms and just hold me and to tell me they care and this too shall pass.

Remember, Job was highly esteemed by our Lord. He did not go through what he did because he was a bad guy, but rather, because he was righteous in God's eyes! God knew he would remain faithful. Job knew that God was in control. He said, "Though He slay me, yet will I hope in Him;" (Job 13:15a). What embarrassment and humiliation He suffered! Yet, he longed for words of encouragement and comfort. Just like you and me. He trusted God, just as Esther trusted

God.

Journaling: Are you thankful in times of affliction? Do you willingly step forth to experience that cleansing fire? Are you seeing the importance of going through the difficult times so He can use you? What does it mean to you to be a faithful servant?

Prayer: Dear Jesus, I thank you for Your love for me, that even in the midst of suffering and pain, You are there. Lord, send someone into my life to be my encourager and friend and point me all the more to You. In Jesus Name…Amen

Personal Challenges:

Day 8

Freedom in the Midst of Struggles

Freedom: liberty, openness, nonconformity, frankness

Scripture reading: Job 2:10; 13:15

I had an Internet chat friend who lived in Australia. Helen was a Godly woman who reached out to people across the miles with her computer. Like Job, she had many struggles in her life. Yet, she had not given up hope, knowing that her life is ruled by God's wisdom and that He knows what is best for her.

Job's faith in the Lord was his source of strength as he experienced heartache after painful heartache. Even when his friends came to comfort him, he was not influenced by their reasoning as to why he suffered great loss of family and material items much less, his health. As we see through today's scripture readings, Job was able to give an answer for his hope.

How did Job gain this sort of faith in God? How do we grow in our faith, even in the midst of our struggles? For surely the Lord wants us to learn and put into practice what He is teaching us throughout Scripture.

We are so privileged to be able to own a Bible and read it as often (or as little) as we want. This is a freedom many do not have! We can also go to our greatest source of love: Jesus. We can give and receive that same love to people and the hurting world because of what Jesus did for us. As we understand what Jesus has done for us, we will want to give that same love to those around us and in return, He allows us to receive love from others. Now, that's freedom!

Freedom is more than living in a country…Freedom is Christ! Freedom is growing in His love. Freedom is giving His love to others!

Journaling: Do you feel free? Free to love the way Jesus loved? Do you feel freedom in the midst of struggles? Freedom to do what God is calling you to do? What is holding you back?

Prayer: Thank you Lord Jesus for giving Yourself as a sacrifice so that I may experience true freedom. In Jesus Name…Amen.

Personal Challenges:

Day 9

The Integrity of Joseph

Integrity: truthfulness, reliable, honest

Scripture reading: Ephesians 4: 17-24; Psalm 139: 23-24

Today I am led to write almost directly from a recent sermon at church and mainly because the subject is Joseph. Truly, Joseph has been a mentor in my life and I hope that he somehow touches your heart and God uses his story to help you grow, as He has me.

We have already discussed a number of struggles that Joseph went through but let's recap. He was hated by his own family. (Gen 37: 4) His brothers were jealous of him. (Gen 37:11) He was sold into slavery (only after they had decided not to kill him). (Gen 37:17-28) He was thrown into prison because of his integrity. (Gen 39:1-20) He was forgotten. (Gen 40:23) Pastor Ryan Guard put it this way, "He was the Forrest Gump of the Bible".

Joseph, a man used by God in his later years, had to suffer plenty along the way. Today I often hear that God gave us hormones, that God created sex and that is the excuse many use to commit adultery. But let us look at the integrity of Joseph. Genesis 39 tells a story of how Joseph was tempted by Potiphar's wife. Not once but twice she approached him and offered him her body...blatantly saying "come to bed with me!"

(Gen 39:7&12) Joseph was a young man (with hormones), handsome and well built. (Gen 39: 6) Potiphar's wife had offered herself to him, yet, he refused her plea both times! (Gen 39: 8; 12)

So, has God given us our body to use for our own pleasure? Or has he given us our body to teach us discipline, integrity, and self control?

If we look to Joseph as our example, we can only conclude that God wants us to be men and women of integrity, not to conform to this world, not to use excuses to sin but to refuse the temptations all around us and to realize that we are not only sinning against God but the other person as well. Yes, God sees and God knows us, better than we know ourselves.

If Joseph would have lived like the world, he would have taken Potiphar's wife up on her offer and would have justified it. After all, it seemed that God had forgotten him, used his brothers to mistreat him and now what an offer! But Joseph showed that he was a decent man, respectful of his master and especially honored his Lord in all he did. He did not justify this offer in any manner.

As you look to the scripture reading for today, see how God can completely make new creations out of each of us. Joseph showed integrity when no one was looking. Who are you when no one is looking?

Journaling: How can you be a person of integrity? Yes, the list could be long, if you have the time, but why not focus on one area at this time. Where is God taking you? How is He showing you His grace through it all?

Prayer: Heavenly Father, You know me, You know my motives, and my innermost thoughts. Show me where I lack integrity and help me in this area. I praise you for Your Word and the honesty of the people so I know I am not alone in my walk. In Jesus Name…Amen

Personal Challenges:

Day 10

Psalm 1:1

Blessed: set apart, consecrated, enjoyed happiness

Scripture reading: James 4:7

The next few days we are going to be looking at Psalm 1. Several years ago, God directed me to write curriculum from Psalm 1 for the students I worked with. Along the way, each of the students taught me a more honest way to live, and moved my heart toward a sincere search for God.

"**Blessed is the man**

who does not walk in the counsel of the wicked

or stand in the way of sinners

or sits in the seat of mockers." (Ps 1:1)

The main idea to the above verse is that people are blessed when they stay away from the wicked, the sinner and mockers. Can you see the progression of one who goes astray? First we will walk towards the wicked person and then we will stop and listen, standing with them. And finally, we will sit down, take a load off our feet and become a part of the group. Walk. Stand. Sit.

When we know that temptation is at the door, we must

think about an escape plan. We make choices to either hang out with the wicked, stand with sinners or take a seat and stay awhile with mockers. Psalm 1 also points out that a person who does not do these things is blessed. The choice is ours.

As we look at the difference between the wicked, the sinner and the mocker we become aware what evil is out there. The wicked have depraved minds that lean towards evil; the sinner is the offender, the wrongdoer, of evil; and the mocker is the person who then bullies those who will not give in to sin. So when we walk in the counsel of people that lean towards evil, our mind becomes corrupt. When we stand in the presence of those who do evil, we are more apt to get caught up in the sin. When we finally move on to sitting with the bully, we do not want to experience their harsh words so we join in to bully others.

In James 4:7 we find good instruction as to how we should handle temptation. It says, "Submit yourselves, then, to God. Resist the devil, and he will flee from you." When we are humble enough to submit to God, we surrender our rights. God only wants what is best for us. Have you ever yielded your life to another person? How about a doctor? Or a parent? Or your boss? Or perhaps the pilot on the plane? Yes, submission is a part of life, we just make a choice as to whom we submit.

Journaling: Now it is your turn, write this verse out and write out how it applies to you. Have you considered who you will walk, stand or sit with? Have you further thought about how you will behave with people you have chosen to be with? Or who you want to run from?

Prayer: Precious Father, I long to be blessed by You!   Help me to learn these lessons of Psalm 1 as quickly as possible and to hold them within my heart and mind so as to never forget Your direction for my life. In Jesus Name...Amen

Personal Challenges:

Day 11

Psalm 1:2

Delight: pleasure, joy, satisfaction

Scripture reading: Psalm 119: 1-35

Psalm 1:2 continues to give direction to the person who wants to be pleasing to the Lord. God has given us such good instructions, if only we would comprehend it, remember it and then do it!

"But his delight is in the law of the Lord and on His Law he meditates day and night." (v2).

The Bible is for all generations and for every situation. Only God could have directed numerous people to have written such a great Book that is concise, speaking to each of us where we are, and meeting our every need.

Several times in our scripture reading today we see a proclamation of the writer's desire and delight in God's decrees, commands or laws. It has been a progression for me as I have read the Bible and remain faithful to this ride in the arms of Jesus. I continue to find daily that, as I read His Word and make a conscience choice to obey it, I feel joy.

Could it be possible that as we are in the Word, we will start reflecting the attitude in which we are influenced? <u>Bible Pathways Ministries</u> gives food for thought, "Yet, it must be obvious from the Word that we measure up spiritually in the eyes of God only as we truly inwardly accept and outwardly express His Word in our daily thoughts and conduct." (July 2011, p30) We need to freely turn our lives in the direction He is guiding us. We do not need to hold on to our past, our bad habits, or our pain, although I often find myself doing just that. Are we delighting in Him?

Journaling: What do you delight in? What is the "law of the Lord"? What does it look like to you to have this sort of delight in His Word? Give an example of how you would apply this verse to your life today.

Prayer: Lord Jesus, how exciting it is to learn that as I take my joy and pleasure in You, You are there to meet me right where I am with opened arms. Hold me Lord, I need you! In Jesus Name…Amen

Personal Challenges:

Day 12

Psalm 1:3

Yield: surrender, produce, earnings, generate

Scripture reading: Psalm 92: 12-15; Jeremiah 17:7-8; John 4:10

When we take a look at Psalm 1:3, we can see the blessings of the person who makes the choice to cherish God's Word.

"He is like a tree planted by streams of water which yields its fruit in season and whose leaf does not wither. Whatever he does prospers." (v3)

I have heard these questions: Does that really mean I have to surrender myself? I feel like I am not my own, that someone is controlling me! Wait, is it different when we surrender our lives to God as versus man?

We had already established that each person is that tree, so I asked each of my students what their tree looked like. One student said that he was a bit withered and dried. Oh how I appreciated his honesty as he took a long look at himself. We then discussed what he needed to do to make his tree become healthy.

As our scripture reading in Psalm 92 points out, we bear fruit even in our old age. We always produce something, whether good or bad, it is fruit. But the Word is Truth and in this Psalm it points out that the "righteous will flourish..." (v 12 and again in v 13). What a wonderful promise! But, this promise comes with stipulations. When we are in His Word, allowing Him to shape us in the way He would have for us to go, then we yield fruit, and we will flourish and prosper!

How in the world does a leaf not wither or not dry up? Earlier we learned that we must have a solid, firm foundation. Today we can see that we can compare ourselves to a well-established tree, whose roots go deep. Once again, we can see that without the Living Water, we are nothing. It is the Living Word that will flow and give us eternal life. But we do have a choice as to where we want to be planted and I am thankful that God has allowed us that choice.

Journaling: Be intentional. Take a look at your tree. Write out how you intend to yield fruit in the next three months. Find a person you can share this with and ask them to help you be accountable. We all need the rain to grow...encouragement is the rain from those around us to help keep us on the right track.

Prayer: Dear Heavenly Father, surrendering myself to you is not a onetime thing, but something I must do daily. Help me to produce fruit that is pleasing to You. In Jesus Name...Amen

Personal Challenges:

Day 13
Psalm 1:4-5

Chaff: coverings on seeds, light jesting talk, mockery

Scripture reading: Psalm 5:5; Psalm 9:8; Psalm 9:16

Today we are going to have a little contrast to that blessed man we have been studying the last few days. Just memorizing this one Psalm can help keep our eyes on Jesus the rest of your days. Let's take a look at the wicked man…what his life is like, not necessarily just here on earth but also in eternity.

"Not so the wicked! They are like chaff that the wind blows away. Therefore the wicked will not stand in the judgment, nor sinners in the assembly of the righteous." (v4-5)

Do you think the wicked have a relationship with God? Are they living to please God or their own desires? If these people do kind acts, do you think they are being kind for others or themselves?

Who is doing the judging? What does God base His judgment on?   The scripture reading for today can be conviction for those who are not walking with Him but for those who are, these verses can be a comfort. In our free-will, we can make a choice to be found among the wicked or among the righteous, it is our choice, our responsibility and we cannot blame anyone else for our choices.

In my own life, I am reminded often of my bad attitude and thoughts and even my bad behavior. That small voice inside is the Holy Spirit reminding me of whom I belong and what I need to do to make things right with God. Yes, even a person who has accepted Christ can be wicked and sinful at times. The difference is when reminded of our stickin' thinkin' or our sinful behavior (either from another person or through His Word, or that small voice), we choose to confess our sinfulness to our Father and then humbly go to the person we have been offensive to and ask their forgiveness as well. Choices, don't you love our Lord for allowing us these choices?

Journaling: Where are you today? Write why you think the wicked will not stand before God. If you have Scripture references, write them down. At some point in your future, you will need this information.

Prayer: Father in Heaven, thank You for showing me where I need to be. Help me Lord, to be pleasing to You and when I do sin, let me be humble enough to confess my sin and want to purge that area of sin out of my life. In Jesus Name…Amen

Personal Challenges:

Day 14

Psalm 1:6

Perish: to completely destroy, to die, to conclude/end

Scripture reading: Psalm 139: 1-16

This conclusion of Psalm 1 can certainly have a double meaning. Now let's take a look at our final verse.

"For the Lord watches over the way of the righteous, but the way of the wicked will perish." (v6)

What happens to the wicked is a frightening thing. They will die. Oh yes, I know we all will die but those who have surrendered themselves to Jesus have a precious promise to never wither, they produce fruit and then, because of eternal life, they will spend eternity with the One who gave them that new life.

Guess what? God knows each of us better than we know ourselves! After contemplating the scripture reading for today, you cannot help but know how much our Lord values you. Psalm 139 also can be a comfort to each of us especially as we need to be reminded often of the blessing that a relationship with God promises.

When I came to the realization that how I live my life each and every day will be a determining factor as to where I will spend eternity, it changed my life. If I say I have accepted Christ as my Savior but continue to

49

live life the same as before, doing or saying hurtful things to others or wanting to argue with people, or being self-centered (you know the list can go on and on), I will be accountable before God one day. Personally, I don't think He will accept my lame excuses for such behavior.

Journaling: Although today's lesson seems short, it is time for you to do some work. Take the time to rewrite all of Psalm 1 in your own words. Personalize it so it becomes your Psalm! If you feel God's leading, memorize it.

Prayer: Heavenly Father, thank you for watching over the righteous. May I be found among them. In Jesus Name...Amen

Personal Challenges:

Day 15

Broken Promises

Promise: guarantee, assure, to give your word, pledge

Scripture reading: Psalm 19: 7-14

Certain times of the day, week, month or year we will make a resolution. We declare we are going to go on a diet and lose weight or we pledge to start exercising or we promise to give more of ourselves to those we love or... the list can go on and on, you add your own resolution. If we can make these promises to ourselves and so easily break them, do we find it easy to break promises to loved ones as well?

Let me tell you a story. A few years ago someone promised that they would teach me to play golf and we would play golf on a regular basis. Well, I am not a very sportsy person so I was excited that someone would want to take the time to teach me this game. In my heart, I looked forward to going golfing. In my mind, I dreamed of that connectedness that I see in the sports world. To make a long story short, it never happened. Each week, and sometimes even mid-week, I watched this person leave for the golf course, never once including me. I even asked if I could go along a time or two and was told this was not the right time. The right time never came...it was a broken promise.

Now, this does not seem like a big promise but I contend that even the smallest of promises made should be kept. When we make a promise to another person and do not keep it, we are actually saying "you are not important enough to me that I would keep my promise to you." I know that sounds pretty drastic but broken marriages or broken friendships often stem from broken promises. We do not value ourselves enough to stay on course and we do not value those around us to do what we have promised them.

Oh, I can hear the excuses right now, for I have said them many times myself. But the truth of the matter is, there is no excuse for breaking a promise! We should not speak the words unless we plan on keeping those words. Even children can have a wounded spirit from the broken promises of adults. If a wounded spirit is not healed, it can lead to bitterness and this takes us on a downward spiral in the relationship. Sad but true!

Journaling: Think about your relationships, have you promised something and not kept it? What can you do about this broken promise? Write it down, pray about it, and then do what needs to be done.

Prayer: Heavenly Father, forgive me for breaking promises to You and to those around me. Help me to keep my word. Lord, help me to forgive those who have broken promises with me. Thank you Lord that You are ever faithful in keeping all Your promises. In Jesus Name…Amen

Personal Challenges:

Day 16

We Need Relationships

Relationship: connection, bond, rapport

Scripture reading: 1 Corinthians 12: 14-26

I know of a woman who got very sick late one summer. Although she was able to continue working, she could do little else. Exhaustion had become a very real part of her life. She once enjoyed talking on the phone or emailing her friends and all of that came to an end as she struggled just to keep her job.

God has made us relational yet millions of Christians each year find themselves in situations where they can hardly function. God is always there by our side. But He also put people on this earth, into our lives because we need each other.

Why then is it that so many find themselves totally alone? They are sick, one way or another, and we are too busy in our own lives to give ourselves to another person. We are drained with our work and families and the thought of bringing another person into our lives that needs us, is almost more than we can endure.

When someone does not answer your phone calls or has not come to church or Sunday school (missing more than a Sunday or two), can we take it upon ourselves to reach out in compassion and love them rather than heap condemnation and wrath upon them? The Scriptures point out that the body is made up of many parts. The church is also a body made up of many parts. When one part of the body is not functioning at full capacity, the rest of the body will suffer.

Now back to our woman in the first paragraph. Oftentimes, hurting people are not capable of reaching out for help. One person that she deemed as a friend, became upset with her when she did not answer her phone and left crushing messages and further added insult to injury by emailing venomous words that only caused the woman to pull further back. The relationships that are to bring the healing and love that God intended have only proven to be hurtful and crushing to her. Yes, both women claim to be Christians. And I'm sure both have been hurt by what has taken place.

It is my hope by telling this story that we will wake up and let Christ lead us in humility, love and compassion and reach out to that person who has withdrawn, that person who has given so much to others but now is unable to do so and that person who is alone with no one to care about them. It is sad that we have so many wounded and dying people within our own realm. Let us not be too busy to even notice.

Journaling: Can you think of someone who would benefit by your call, note or email? Make a list of people and jot down something you can do for each of them. Yes, you guessed it, then do it.

Prayer: Father, thank you for caring so deeply for me, meeting my every need. Thank you for putting people in my life in which I can reach out and give them love. Show me who you want me to touch today. In Jesus Name...Amen

Personal Challenges:

Day 17

Suffering

Suffer: endure, bear, experience, go through

Scripture reading: 2 Corinthians 12: 7-10; Philippians 1:29

Did you know there are people who cannot tolerate life in a society saturated with chemicals and toxins? Their bodies react adversely to perfumes, plastics, carpeting, gases, paints, resins, synthetic fabrics, beauty products, household cleansers, bug spray, and weed killers that most people take for granted, as well as many different foods, molds, pollens, and dust. This isn't an all-inclusive list, there is always something new coming out. Some cannot tolerate electromagnetic fields from cell phones/towers, computers, appliances, etc. Yes, it is true! I am one of those people.

Each of us have different reactions to exposures, varying in intensity and for a number of years, we were told that it was all in our heads. These exposures can affect every organ system in the body, causing a myriad of physical, mental and emotional symptoms. The reactions can also be ongoing or delayed, causing chronic symptoms as in the case of Chronic Fatigue Syndrome, Fibromyalgia, and Gulf War Syndrome (at least the medical profession has finally come up with names for these).

Having suffered from Environmental Illness for over 25 years, I have learned to go to the Great Physician when no one else could help me or believe my pain. Headaches that send me to bed for days, pain in my body so severe that I cannot function, a melancholy gloominess hanging over me without warning are just a few of the symptoms I experience. In 1983 I became aware that my environment was causing me to be sick and for about six months I lived in my bedroom next to an air purifier. We had to get rid of all the bedroom furniture because it contained formaldehyde so I slept on the floor. I ate one food per meal, three foods per day and 21 foods per week to figure out the offending foods in my life. There was very little known at that time about E.I.

Today people are more aware of those who suffer like this but prayer is always appreciated. I would also add, pray for a safe church as well. We need the spiritual food and fellowship too!

I pleaded with Him for healing but as I pored over scripture, I realized that many suffer and that we all suffer one way or another. In fact, it is those who go through these hard times that God can use the most for they have no hope in anyone or anything but Him. Is God calling you to minister to this hurting group of people? Maybe you are hurting, you are suffering, not from EI but something just as devastating to you. There are times when He picks you up and holds you in His strong arms. There are times when He allows suffering so someone can come along side you and take some of your burden. Persevere, dear one!

Journaling: Do you know someone who is sensitive to scented products or other chemicals? Is it possible for you to reach out to them in some special way? Write out a list and a way you can minister to them.

Prayer: Lord, I lift up people who suffer. I ask Lord, that you would provide a safe place for them to live and also an understanding church that is willing to meet their special needs. In Jesus Name…Amen

Personal Challenges:

Day 18

Self Examination

Examine: scrutinize, inspect, study, to investigate

Scripture reading: Psalm 139: 17-24

As I mature in my Christian walk, I am learning to examine myself more than I examine others. In fact, our scripture reading today encourages us to do this.

What brought David to his knees as he prayed for God to examine not only his outward behavior but his inward thoughts and motives? What caused David to want to know whether he had offensive ways, or that his behavior had caused pain to God or to his fellow man?

Perhaps we can better understand David's heartfelt prayer by further examining what he said right before his prayer at the end of Psalm 139. It is interesting that many will quote the first part of this Psalm showing how God has searched us and knows us so intimately and that He knows our thoughts. Also verse 13 is well known of how God created us in our mother's womb.

Seldom have I heard a sermon on verses 19-22, where David's enemies are seen as God's enemies. I suspect that David saw their fruit: how they talked, how they behaved, their attitudes towards God and man, and made such a judgment. He counted God's enemies as his enemies and desired God's righteous justice, not personal revenge. It is then that David went into self examination.

He asked God to investigate his heart and to do exploratory surgery, so to speak, to the depth of his thought life. David wanted God to reveal any sin in him so that he might confess it and turn away from it.

Do the sins of those around us make us sick to our stomach or do we accept them, laugh with them and join in? Do we love people enough to point them to God's Word for the truth that will set them free? We can only do that after self-examination!

If you are seeking God for answers and you say, "He doesn't seem to be giving me answers", perhaps you are looking in the wrong place. The Bible does have all the answers. It is the truth, the whole truth and nothing but the truth. When we are not doing our part it is hard to get answers from the Lord.

We need to spend more time in the Word of God than in other books, magazines, or playing video games or watching TV. We need to be careful what our eyes look at, what our minds are pondering upon and where our focus is. Ask Him what he wants to teach you this day.

Journaling: Write down at least one thing you can do concerning examining yourself. If God has shown you an area that needs improvement or change, write out how you intend to do that.

Prayer: O God, I do ask that you would delve into the depth of my heart and my mind. Show me where there is sin in my life and help me to change and be the person that brings glory to You.   In Jesus Name…Amen

Personal Challenges:

Day 19

Resolve to Change Your Heart

Resolve: determination, firmness, doggedness

Scripture reading: James 1:22; 1 John 2:16; Ephesians 4:28

Does God ever speak to you through His Word and you eagerly desire to soak it in to the depth of your very being? Sometimes, don't you just wish you could absorb what He is saying to you by having it become part of your practical everyday life? Deeply desiring to do His will to the point that your heart aches?

James says that what I set my heart on, I will do. I don't know about you but I read God's Word, yet I do not always carry out what I read, even though I have good intentions. I must daily resolve to stop feeding my own cravings, whether the flesh, or lust of the eyes or that pride that swells inside me. One way we can be successful in changing an old habit is replacing the old habit with a new habit, something superior to take its place.

Just as Eve set her eyes on that piece of fruit, we set our eyes on (you fill in the blank), and we only have our own interests in mind. We then start to question God's Word. We even come up with scriptural excuses why we should fulfill that desire. We can see another progression taking place here: first we fulfill the cravings of the flesh with our eyes and then must satisfy the physical desire. We feed our mind with more justification as to why God would want us to have that piece of fruit, now we are ready to move on. After all God is a loving God and He would want us to have it, right?

We have just gone through the steps of the lures of Satan. He baited us and now he is reeling us in. Does any of this sound familiar? Surely I am not the only one who has fallen into his trap!

Dr. Jay Adams, in his book The Christian Counselor's Manual, suggests that sin for many of us has become a way of life, second nature (if you will). In order to have a behavioral change, we must have a heart change.

So, as we resolve to change a habit, let us remember that we are changing a habit that needs a Godly replacement. Change takes time, we will fail on occasion but don't let that failure discourage you. Persevere until the habit is changed, giving glory to God who has given you the answers and the strength.

By the way, God does expect His children to change, to become more like Him. And, it is possible with His help! Find a person to whom you can be accountable, someone who will encourage you and pray for and with you. Keep your goals realistic and scriptural and do not expect yourself to change too many things at one time. I am right there with you, let's walk this road together!

Journaling: Can you name one area in which you need to change? Can you think of a Godly, scriptural replacement? Pray for God's help to change your heart and mind; then take your first step towards a new life in Christ.

Prayer: Precious Heavenly Father, I want to change but cannot do it without You. Guide me each step of the way, pick me up when I get discouraged or fail and give me the desire to become more like Jesus. In Jesus Name…Amen

Personal Challenges:

Day 20

The Ride of a Lifetime

Ride: journey, traverse, be carried

Scripture reading: Mark 8:38; Hebrews 12: 1-2

Several verses come to mind as I ask the Lord, "What would You have me share?", so be sure and read the scriptures suggested for today.

I am reminded that as we draw closer to Him, attacks will come, discouragement will come and suffering will come. John Avant, in his book Authentic Power, shares with us what our response should be, "Instead of focusing our prayers against any political system, we pray that regardless of what happens to us, we will be pleasing to God. Don't pray for the persecution to stop! We shouldn't pray for a lighter load to carry but a stronger back to endure! Then the world will see that God is with us, empowering us to live in a way that reflects His love and power." (p 65)

Do we hunger to know Christ so deeply that we are willing to pray for a stronger back? We do not have to die as a martyr to share in his suffering, but we must be willing to die to self. Die to self…just exactly what does that mean? Perhaps it means giving up a part of yourself that you have held on to saying, "that's just the way I am." Or perhaps it is giving a part of yourself away to a loved one, giving up your rights and showing them how much you really care. Or perhaps it is giving some of your precious time to His work. Dying to self is oftentimes painful but as you give yourself to Him, your awareness of His presence is made stronger. People will be able to see a little more of Christ in you. Yes, you will bear the fruit of being like Christ. And believe me, we are to examine ourselves and each other on our journey to become more Christ-like. We are to find that accountability partner, who knows you so well and loves you enough to help guide you (one another) along the tough road that lies ahead.

This walk through life becomes an exciting ride with Him who has known you since you were conceived and is there beside you each step of the way. When the journey becomes tough, He is there to carry you until you've gained strength once again.

I know the journey isn't always easy but have you considered that by not going forward to accept Him as your personal Savior, or not seeing the importance of obedience according to scripture, or not searching His Word daily and asking "what's next, Lord?" or not seeing the importance of suffering, then you cannot mature in Christ. Each of us walks our own path but we need the encouragement of another person along the way. We need at least one person to come along side us and care enough to show us in love where we can change.

As we focus on Jesus, looking straight into the His eyes, are we ready to stand firm in Him? Why don't we take that step together?

Journaling: Are you ready for the ride of a

lifetime? Are you ready to make those changes in your life that are needed? Are you ready to die to self, no matter how painful it is?

Prayer: Lord, help me to never deny You but to always keep my eyes on You. I am ready for the next step, show me the way. In Jesus Name...Amen

Personal Challenges:

Day 21

I Stand in Awe of Your Deeds, O Lord...

Awe: wonder, fear, respect, admiration

Scripture reading: Habakkuk 2:4-5; 3:19

In those moments of great despair, when I feel so defeated, I need to be reminded of His awesome deeds. That reminder comes from His Word and our Christian brothers and sisters. God made us to be relational, to have deep and meaningful relationships with one another. Then the hopelessness that we sometimes feel can be shared and encouragement can abound.

When it seems that God is tolerating wrong and destruction and violence is all around, we must remember God's answer to Habakkuk. God knows! Our Lord knows our pain and agony but also knows our hearts can be arrogant and full of pride. He knows we can be greedy creatures, only looking out for ourselves. He knows we must go through certain happenings in order to get our attention so that we will want to change. Truly, to grasp that He allows those good and bad times in our lives so as to draw us closer to the heart of Christ is an awesome wonder.

I have just finished reading through the Old Testament and must tell you each year God shows me yet another area of His power and love and how He is molding me into the person He wants me to be. Each year as I read through the Bible, I see something significant at that time. I have to laugh at myself because I will say something like, "I've never seen that in the Bible before" knowing full well that I read it last year and the year before. Our awesome God opens my sinful eyes and mind to yet another area in which I need to grow.

As an example, the first time I read through the Bible, I was shocked at how the Israelites could so easily turn from God. My spiritual journey was just beginning. Through the years, the Lord has shown me how easily I can turn away from Him and go my own way. In repentance, I have gone before Him many times, and He is there, waiting for me with open arms! As I stay in his Word daily, He renews me.

Bible Pathways says, "The Book of Habakkuk encourages all believers to accept by faith every situation, trusting that righteousness and justice will ultimately triumph according to the righteous judgment of the One True God." (Sept 2005, p 39). Can I accept by faith every situation? Every situation? Habakkuk also reminds me that all those hurtful situations I have experienced are a part of God's Divine plan. He expects me to learn from them, let go of the pain and bondage and reach out to other hurting people.

Together, let us declare how God has gotten each of us through those tough times and how He has enabled us to take the next step. Let us together stand in awe that our Lord would love us so much as to use us as He does.

Journaling: How many times in recent days have you looked at your life and stood in awe before the Lord? Take time today to journal the awesomeness of the Lord, those marvelous works He is doing in your life.

Prayer: Father God, who am I that You should care so much for me as to reveal Yourself in all that I am and all that I do? I am thankful for the mercy and strength You give me each day. In Jesus Name…Amen

Personal Challenges:

Day 22

Saying Yes Can Change Your Life Forever

Yes: agree, of course, sure

Scripture reading: Isaiah 6:5-8; Luke 1:37-38; James 5:7-9; 2 Corinthians 12:7-10

Are we as willing as many of the people of the Bible were to say yes to the Lord? Do we enter His presence in fear of the One True God? When Isaiah was experiencing the presence of the Lord, he realized his own filthiness and yet he, like so many others, answered God's call with a willing heart.

As we read the Bible, we will be reminded over and over that nothing is impossible with God. Yet, what has He asked you to do that you see as impossible? Do you think that a young, virgin named Mary, could even imagine being pregnant, not having been with a man? Or had she thought through what would be expected of her in raising the Son of God? Finally, could she have known the pain of seeing her son die on a cross? Yet, she said yes to God. What a faithful woman she was!

Drawing closer to Christ is a process but it also takes strong faith to step out and say "Yes Lord, I will do_____." You fill in the blank for He calls each of us to a different task. What may seem easy to one will be of the utmost difficulty to another. It is not for us to look at someone else's calling and think that would be so much better or easier than what God has called me to do. And when God calls us, we must look at it as a precious gift from the One who knows us completely, who knows what we need so as to grow more in His way. If we come into serving Him with a wrong attitude, He will use it. But none the less, it will be a harder, a more painful journey.

Whatever He's called you to do, just know that God expects us to persevere and to not complain! Along the way, we gain practical holiness and spiritual maturity and sometimes this is the painful part. He knows us so completely that He calls us, oftentimes, in the weak areas of our lives so we can depend upon Him totally.

When we first meet Paul in Acts (his name is still Saul at that point), he is a leader, a man of strength, a man who stands for what he believes in. God saw those strengths and wanted to use Paul but along the way, he went through a few beatings, a stoning or two, and rejection from his former friends and sometimes from those he was preaching to. He suffered in ways that only God knows but I think that his viewpoint in 2 Corinthians 12 speaks of a new man different from the one God first called.

Years ago when I got very sick and I had people around me telling me that I must have some "sin" in my life, otherwise God would heal me; God used these verses to sooth those fiery words. God showed me that when a person is not healed, He is using that time to mold the person to become more like Christ. That is exactly what I needed.

The results of saying "yes" to the Lord will involve quite an adventure, if you are willing to accept His calling. As you are reading the Word daily, you will grasp the blessings that await you but you will also start to understand that we serve a God who is loving and He will allow the good and the bad to come into our lives. He uses all circumstances, even suffering and pain, to build our character into the person He knew we would be all along.

It is an exciting quest each and every step of the way! Saying "yes" will change your life. Saying "yes" will help you become the person that the Lord will welcome into the kingdom. Salvation comes from Jesus death, burial and resurrection...but once we've experienced what He's done for us, we will have a longing within us to serve Him and those around us.

Journaling: Does it seem harder to say yes to the Lord when you feel that the area He has called you is not one of your strong points? Take some time and journal your thoughts as to what God is calling you to and whether you are willing.

Prayer: Lord Jesus, thank you for trusting me even when I cannot see that saying yes to you will be of any benefit. Help me Lord to always stay on course and be willing to serve You, no matter what You call me to do. In Jesus Name...Amen

Personal Challenges:

Day 23

Good Stewardship

Steward: overseer, supervisor, custodian

Scripture reading: Matthew 6:21 & 33

The word budget almost seems like a dirty word in this modern world. In fact, people who work in finances have given it a new name: it is a spending plan. Truly, whatever you want to call it, start one if you don't have one and if you are on a budget, stick to it. At any rate, learning this new discipline of using God's money is exciting.

About ten years ago, I worked with a family who was in financial trouble. Most people that I have worked with on budgeting get into trouble because they use credit cards to spend beyond what they make. So, this family cut those credit cards up in my presence and sign a contract saying that for at least the next six month, they would not use a credit card. Also, we started this process in October so that didn't leave much budget money for Christmas gifts.

The family was encouraged to stick to what little money they had and became very creative in their Christmas giving. When I met with them in January, they told me it was the "best Christmas we have ever had". Why, you may ask because I certainly did? Well, first of all, they didn't have any debt to pay after Christmas and secondly, they saw their children enjoy simple homemade gifts. They had bought one of the children a slinky for 99 cents and that became the whole family's enjoyment for weeks afterwards. This family was learning the excitement of disciplining themselves.

Simplicity and creativity in giving can bring more joy to your heart and your family than spending money (that you don't have) on expensive toys that leave the child wanting something more or enjoying the box more than the gadget.

Please don't get me wrong. I am not saying that credit cards of themselves are evil but the misuse of credit cards will cause big problems in the long run. For many, as they crawl out of debt, they see that a budget and working to be debt-free is very comforting compared to the life they were living before.

The late Larry Burkett wrote in <u>The Coming Economic Earthquake</u> that financial depression doesn't just happen but is the conclusion of decades of irresponsibility. I might add that it doesn't matter whether it is the government or the people, we must all do our part. As we look at what has happened in our society in recent years, we too must be reminded that there has been economic abuse for quite some time.

I recently heard on a radio program about a meeting of world leaders that had come to the conclusion concerning the latest economic downfall. They claimed it had started in New York, so they, as world leaders, must set up stops points to keep from having a total collapse. They used the words "a new economic world order" as the way out of this financial situation.

Well that perked up my ears. Do we really need world leaders "handling" the economic problems or do we need people who have decided to become responsible in their spending?

Each of us needs encouragement to continue staying on a budget and to get out of debt! We need to feel the freedom of living a life with no debt. Think about it, can you imagine no longer being controlled by excessive spending? It is a wonderful feeling to have control and it gives you the freedom to give more. Truly, it is exciting times as we concentrate on serving the Lord in every area of our lives!

Be encouraged as you make those changes and choose to stay on that budget, working towards being debt-free. If you are already there, give generously to the Lord's work and perhaps helping someone who is in need, as the Lord directs. We can truly be thankful in the One to whom we put our trust.

Journaling: Are you on a budget? If not, are you interested in getting control of that area of your life? Journal the possibilities of your next step. 1. Take a class to learn how to budget. 2. Read a book on budgeting. 3. Seek out a person who will come alongside you to help you with the necessary steps in budgeting.

Prayer: Father, you have given me all that I have. Help me to learn how to be a good steward of what you have given me so that You will be glorified. In Jesus Name...Amen

Personal Challenges:

Day 24

Once In a Blue Moon

Once: formerly, on one occasion, when

Scripture reading: Deuteronomy 23:23; Numbers 30:2

Have you heard the saying "once in a blue moon" when someone is describing something that doesn't happen often? Did you know that a second full moon in the month is called a blue moon? It only happens about once every two and a half years. So, the phrase "once in a blue moon" usually means 'not very often'. For all of those promises made, the next blue moon is the time to collect and/or keep the promises we have made.

This is an important area of any Christian's life: to be true to your word, to carry through and do what you say you will do. I know I fall short in this area. I tell someone I will do something and by the time I get home, I have forgotten about it. I have good intentions but do not carry through with those intentions. Once in a blue moon I actually remember one of those promises and do it.

How can I change my behavior in this area? If I were accountable to someone on a regular basis, they could ask me if I have kept my promises. Remember, I don't have to say "I promise to do…" to have the person take it as such. I must also remember that when I do not keep my word, that can be cause for the other person not to trust me (even over the small things).

A father promises to take his children to the park Saturday afternoon but the night before he gets a call from a friend who lives out of town and he doesn't see often. This friend can only see him Saturday afternoon, that's the only time he has available. This father thinks his children will understand and makes the arrangements to see his friend. That father has broken his promise to his children and this simple act could cause his children to feel rejected, or that he does not value them, or can even cause bitterness to grow within them.

So, in this time of spiritual growth, let us make a special effort to go back and get that "honey do" list caught up. Let's get in gear and keep those promises we have made to the Lord. Maybe that includes reading the Word daily or a new Bible study. Maybe it means being involved in serving the people around you. Maybe it's doing something special with a loved one (and they have been waiting a long time).

Perhaps God will use this time to bring someone close to you into the full knowledge of Christ and they will invite Jesus into their heart. God is a God of miracles and I know He uses all circumstances to collect those promises made. I need to be keenly aware of what I say and know that God expects me to act upon my words. What about you?

Journaling: Is there a promise you have made to someone that still needs to be done? Ask God to help you to remember these promises and be sure to apologize that it has taken you so long to fulfill it.

Prayer: Lord, Help me to fulfill my promises to others and keep me ever mindful that You always keep Your promises to me. Thank you Jesus …Amen

Personal Challenges:

Day 25

Trust in the Lord

Trust: confidence, expectation, dependence, reliance

Scripture reading: Proverbs 3:5; John 14:1

All too often, I grieve over what might have been. I hold on to the past instead of moving forward. King David did this when his son Absalom was killed. This greatly confused the troops!

Absalom had his half-brother, Amnon, killed and then he conspires to take over his father's kingdom. Do you get the picture? David grieved over his son, over what might have been. I grieve over things in the past and what might have been. I often hold on way too long. But Paul tells us in Phil. 3:13-14, "Forgetting what is behind and straining toward what is ahead, I press on toward the goal to win the prize for which God has called me heavenward in Christ Jesus." We see this throughout scripture and we experience it today.

What causes the "what might have been" mentality? Is it arrogance on our part? Or perhaps it is a defiant attitude, that we know better than God (although maybe we don't think of it in quite those terms)? Is it just a lack of trusting the Lord? As we are now on day 25 in this devotional in search of God to fill the emptiness within our soul, we start to understand that God is in control. Nothing happens in our lives that

He does not allow to happen. Yes, we make bad choices at times, and He uses those choices for our good. Often it may take us years before we can see His purpose, but remember, there is always a purpose.

As we keep our focus on Jesus and daily read, comprehend and believe the Truth, which is the Bible, He will help us to not dwell on the past but to look forward to the future. A future in which we know we are exactly where God wants us and are ready and willing to serve Him.

Journaling: What are you being called to this very day? What must you let go of in order for this to happen? Make a plan and take that first step towards moving forward and not living in the past.

Prayer: Father in Heaven, I trust in Your Word and know You keep watch over me. Help me to remember daily that you care for me and love me deeply and that you will not let anything happen to me that You are not directing the course. In Jesus Name...Amen

Personal Challenges:

Day 26

Challenged to Growth

Growth: increase, expansion, progress

Scripture reading: Hebrews 4:12; Psalm 119:105

There was a man who maintained the status of "Christian" because he goes to a men's Bible Study and goes to church regularly and yet says he cannot read the Bible. He claims that he does not get anything out of the Bible but listens to preachers on the radio and that should be good enough. Do you agree? Is it enough?

If Hebrews 4:12 is true, then reading God's Word has to speak to you. Perhaps this man isn't reading a version of the Bible that is understandable or perhaps his heart is not right. I am not to judge beyond what scripture says. Do you think this man is producing fruit? The Word cannot help but change you as you seek to do God's perfect will. We cannot know what God's will is if we are not reading/comprehending what He has written.

I believe the Word of God is the very core of one's moral and spiritual life. It will produce change in our lives as we read it. It is only through our actions that we can show the world who we belong to. As the Holy Spirit quickens our spirit and helps us to discern good and evil in our own lives, we will want to modify our behavior to align with His Word. His Word is safety to us, showing us the way ahead. It shows us where we have fallen short in our behavior and our thoughts. It is the only Way to stay on the right path in bringing glory to God in our words, thoughts and behavior.

Do you know the Word of God well enough to know that the man in the example is not alone? As we read through the Bible, we see time after time an attitude of indifference to the Lord and His teaching. We see people who think they are spiritual but are far away from the truth of God. Yes, in the Word we see these examples and yes, in our everyday life we will run across the same.

As you take the challenge to give God priority in your life, you can only imagine how God will honor you. He will show you answers to your struggles in life. He will guide you into a better understanding as to how to live your life for Him. You will start to gain wisdom!

For one person, they will read through the Bible yearly, following a set schedule. For another person, God will guide them to focus on certain Scripture in depth. For yet another, God will guide them through a devotional. We are all different but we all need the Word of God … it is our Guide for Great Living!

Journaling: Are you feeling challenged when it comes to reading the Bible? Do you struggle with understanding what it says? Do you need to read a different version of the Bible, one that you can comprehend?

Prayer: Dear Lord, help me to understand Your

Word.   I need to daily read the Bible so I can be pleasing to you. Thank you for allowing me to have a Bible to read. In Jesus Name…Amen

Personal Challenges:

Day 27

Growing Pains

Pain: grief, tenderness, anguish, sorrow

Scripture reading: Lamentations 4:2

Scripture memorization can be very discouraging, especially as we get older. I find what once took me five minutes a day and five to seven days to memorize now takes me 20 minutes a day for seven to 30 days for one single verse! This, no doubt, can be very demoralizing!

As I shared with you earlier, the Psalm 1 curriculum I wrote was a challenge for the students (and for me). Not only did the students have to memorize the Scripture but we looked at the meaning of words, they had to find the main idea or principle of the verse and finally each student searched their own heart to see how to apply the verse to their daily lives.

Often we do not expect this sort of depth out of ourselves, let alone a child. But scripture memorization is so much easier for a child and I believe that as we use scripture to teach our children, God will honor these children in ways that will only be understood in years to come.

I work with students who struggle in their learning. Most of them are brilliant in certain areas but have deficit areas as well. It was not too many months into working with such students that I realized that each of us has some sort of deficit area. Some people are prone to pretend there is nothing wrong while others use their deficit area to manipulate those around them. And still others want to conquer this insufficiency and move on (these were my students and their parents).

I believe that those who struggle are chosen by God for God uses hardships in our lives so that we will depend on Him. He uses adversity in our lives to mold us and strengthen us. He knows what each of us needs and what we can handle to prepare us for what lies ahead.

These areas of struggle are God's way of showing us how much we need Him. We need to learn to be flexible, to listen to what God is telling us, to be willing to change and become a person whose sole desire is to please the Father. Often times, this is a painful process but well worth it in the end.

What verse or verses of Scripture is God calling you to memorize? As you memorize, let the Words soak into your very being and become a part of you. His lessons are perfect!

Journaling: Do you see within yourself an area of struggle? Are you willing to allow the Lord to use this area for His glory? Start a list of verses you want to memorize and start the memorization process, hiding His Word in your heart.

Prayer: Heavenly Father, memorization isn't always easy for me so I ask that you would give me the desire to memorize your Word and to use it in my daily life. In Jesus Name…Amen

Personal Challenges:

Day 28

Fear and Reverence

Revere: admire, respect, worship

Scripture reading: Psalm 112:1; Proverbs 1:7; 1 Peter 2:17;

When we have a healthy fear of God, we are set free to lead a fearless life. That seems to be contradictory of our Christian teaching these days. I have heard for many years that we are to have "no fear" of God, and in that, I am fearful for those who say such a thing.

As we take on that dose of healthy fear of the Lord, He releases us of our own personal fears. I used to say I would die of fright. I was afraid of the dark. I was afraid of many people. I was afraid of strangers. I was afraid of new experiences. Well, you have the basic picture, don't you?

About 20 years ago, I memorized John 14:27 (KJV) "Peace I leave with you, My peace I give unto you: not as the world giveth, give I unto you. Let not your heart be troubled, neither let it be afraid." When I would get up at night and walk through a dark house, I would quote that verse to myself. I even said it out loud! Through the years, I have quoted it and God has brought me through the fear. My heart does not fear and I (most of the time) am not afraid. I can walk through a dark house or into a roomful of strangers for my God is with me. When I find myself fearful, I know I need to call out to the One who can take that fear away.

But on the other hand, my fear of the Lord has grown as the years go by. By being in the Word daily, praying continually, being joyful, giving thanks in all circumstances, I am learning, slowly, that the Lord Jesus is my advocate. He is my encourager, my supporter in times of fearful situations! What can mere man do to me that God does not see?

As we give Him the first part of our time each day, He takes our fears, one by one, and lifts the burdens. As a result, our load gets lighter and we become more loving, generous and have a desire to "carry" our fellow man and the burdens what weigh upon them.

To fear the Lord is a "fountain of life" (Pro 14:27) and it "leads to life" (Pro 19:23). To fear man and this world "will prove to be a snare" (Pro 29:25a). Adam only had fear after he sinned, "I heard You in the garden, and I was afraid…" (Gen 3:10). You see, we are all sinners. No matter where we are on our journey, we will sin. Unless we are in the Word and listening to the Holy Spirit, we can become proud. But as we fear and revere our Lord, He will give us a strength that can only come from Him. And thus, my journey is deepening in my love and respect for Him!

Journaling: How have you been taught concerning fearing the Lord? Do a word study to gain a better understanding of the importance to fear the Lord. Write out your ideas and thoughts concerning a healthy dose of fear for the Lord.

Prayer: Heavenly Father, help me to grasp that fearing You is good; help me to have a healthy respect for Who You are, not only a Loving Father but also Judge of the universe. In Jesus Name…Amen

Personal Challenges:

Day 29

Holiness Brings Happiness

Holy: sacred, righteous, pure, virtuous

Scripture reading: 1 Peter 1:15-16; 1 Peter 3:7

I once attended the "Iron Couples Conference", the featured speaker was Gary Thomas, a man I had never heard of before, but I am so glad that I was able to hear him speak as he challenged me to focus on changing myself to become more Christ-like.

No matter what relationship we look at, it is easy to see the other person's faults and see where they need to change. Gary introduced a concept that was new to me: God's design concerning marriage (I think any relationship) is not so much for our happiness but to bring us to holiness. It is through our interaction with one another that our weaknesses are brought out. We have a choice to change those weaknesses (through the power of Christ) or continue in those weaknesses with the excuse, "that's just the way I am".

Much of what Gary shared in the three messages is found in his book Sacred Marriage. Yes, I bought the book and read it. In Gary's messages as well as his book, he is straight forward in confronting us with Biblical truths. I cannot even tell you how many times Ephesians 5:25-31 was quoted in one form or another. The men were admonished to "love their wives as Christ loved the church and gave Himself up for her to make her holy…". And the women were reminded how important respect is. Most importantly, we are reminded to submit to one another in order to show respect to Christ (see verse 21).

God uses our marriage partner to expose our sin. Look at Adam and Eve and how their sin brought about a breakdown in marital intimacy and they started blaming each other. God is still using relationships to expose our sin and we are still blaming each other and marriages continue to have a breakdown in intimacy. I once heard that intimacy is spelled "T-A-L-K". How is it spelled in your opinion?

Have you thanked God for that special person He has given you? When our sin comes out in full force, we need to be humble enough to repent. Repentance is acknowledging our sin, for nothing can change unless we recognize our evil, and then turn away from it. Who better has God put in our lives than a spouse (or a very close friend, if you are not married) who can see our sin and our struggles, then help us change and encourage us along the way?

Also in Gary's book, he challenges us to see the importance of prayer concerning marriage. Not only is prayer essential for our marriages but if husbands are not treating their wives right, God does not even hear their prayers. Again, we see that God uses marriage as well as other relationships to refine us and to draw us closer to Him as we strive to be holy through living holy lives.

We all fall short but when we sin, grab your partner's hand and determine to remain humble as you seek

Christ and become more like Him, together. If you are single, Jesus is that someone who will love you enough to take you on this new journey.

Journaling: Write down the name of the person with whom you can be transparent with. Determine what area in your life needs a facelift and then start the task. Be sure to write down your progress and how your spouse or friend can help you.

Prayer: Father, help me to see that the only way I am going to be happy is by living a holy life. Help me each and every day to break down the walls of pride and let me live for You! In Jesus Name…Amen

Personal Challenges:

Day 30

Pick and Choose

Choose: decide, prefer, desire, elect

Scripture reading: Matthew 12:36; 1 Corinthians 12

Throughout life we have choices to make. Whether they are our friendships, the type of food we eat, how we exercise, or how deep we allow our relationships to be, these choices are of great value. They will certainly influence us and those around us for many years.

We can choose to accept Christ into our lives but never learn from the teachings the Bible has to offer. Or we can study these teachings but never put them into practice. We can pick and choose Scripture to fit our needs but never allow the Lord's intended purpose for those Scriptures to work in our lives. Yes, we always have choices.

There are check-points, if we allow them, in our lives that help us to grow in Christ. Bible studies with a group of people, a Bible study with one or two close friends, or we can find accountability with a spouse or a very dear friend. We need someone who will encourage us and love us even when we fall…and to believe in us, despite our shortcomings and failures.

No matter what body of believers we belong, we will have people within the body that we can go to, count on and receive love. We also need to be people who others can come to, count on and give love. We need such relationships to challenge one another to live what we have declared.

You are a special gift that God has brought to fellowship where you are now worshipping. You are either a missionary or a mission field, or sometimes we can be both at the same time. As we open up to one another, we need to learn to be vulnerable and have humility. Both of these character qualities are needed in order to take a relationship to a deeper, more meaningful level.

Whatever God is calling you to do in serving the body of Christ, you still have choices. You can grasp that calling or you can reject it. You can admit that you yourself need support from others and you can be willing to give support or you can take the road of being alone and not expose your inner self to anyone. Some see that as a safe route, as I sometimes do.

Whether your marriage or a friendship needs deeper intimacy, just know you make the choice to take the time to become bonded with another person. Deeper intimacy happens as you share your heart and soul with one another person. Deeper intimacy is hard work! Even if we make the choice to not get involved in the church or with another human being, we must live with those choices. The consequences are being alone, being self-centered and experiencing God's judgment. Our scripture reading for today helps us to see that God is not only a God of love but a God who will one day judge. I suppose that would also include careless actions as well.

God has also given us a special gift. Each other! In

serving the Lord, we serve others and I am so thankful for <u>you</u>.

Journaling: Whom will you serve today? Are you in a church who wants to use your talents? Find out what is needed in your church and make yourself available. If you are not involved in a church, find a church that needs you.

Prayer: Thank you Jesus for allowing me to pick and choose but help me to be willing to serve You starting today. In Jesus Name...Amen

Personal Challenges:

Day 31

Washing

Wash: cleanse, tint, bear

Scripture reading: Ephesians 2:8-10; James 2:24; 1 John 1:9-10; 2 Corinthians 5:17

I once read a quote from Martin Luther, "The unwillingness of the sinner to be regarded as a sinner is the final form of sin." I think this is a pretty powerful statement and it helps me to keep myself in check as well as to understand why my heart breaks when someone sins but does not see it as sin.

Then I have to ask myself, *"why don't we see sin as sin?"*

The only answer I can come up with is we do not know the Word or we don't want to know the Word. We are talking about Christians as well as those who don't call themselves Christian. The more we familiarize ourselves with the Word of God...every word, from cover to cover...the more we will think in a Christian Worldview, the more we will grasp the principles that God is trying to teach us and the more we are likely to put those principles into actions.

So, we are saved by faith, not by works, but as we read the Bible, we will develop a deep desire to obey and serve. We serve by putting what we've read into action. The Bible is the most exciting book I have ever read. Not only does it stimulate my mind and heart but each time I read through it, God directs me in a different way and I learn something new. Something that was already there, but I wasn't ready for the lesson. New principles, new lessons given by God are there for our learning. There is one stipulation: I must read the Word He has given me and then work hard in doing it. I know how I've grown and want you to experience it too.

When I read such a profound statement as Martin Luther's, I know Luther was a man who was in the Word. For such a bold statement could only come from the Bible as we have seen in our scripture readings for today. Each and every day, we need to recognize our sins, confess them and move on. Those who do not recognize they have sinned still live in their sins.

The people in the Old Testament were "Biblically illiterate" and of course, they did not have the Bible as we do today. God spoke to them through His prophets. When there was a revival, the people would listen to God's law, discuss God's law and understand how God's laws could change them. Throughout the OT we see a stubborn people who repented and lived for God and then turned away and did their own thing. In my life, I know I have done that as well. I pray that I don't ever become so hardened that I do not recognize when I sin, being willing to go before God with a repentant heart and go to the person I've sinned against and ask for forgiveness.

As we read (or listen to) God's Word, we will realize (through the Holy Spirit) how essential it is for our daily living. We are to remain faithful to God and through this washing away our old thoughts and ways, we truly can become a new creation.

Journaling: What struck you right between the eyes in today's reading? Journal where you are in your Christian walk.

Prayer: Heavenly Father, may my worldview be so established in Your Word that my every word and action can be traced back to the only Truth there is, the Bible! In Jesus Name…Amen

Personal Challenges:

Day 32

Be Filled...

Fill: to fill up, to saturate, to satisfy

Scripture reading: Galatians 5:22-23; Colossians 3:12-17

What is our responsibility in the history making moment of elections? Mostly, people tell you to get out there and vote and I agree with that. We are privileged in the United States in that we have the freedom to elect the officials who rule over us. But often times, we have no idea who we really are voting for. With this dilemma at hand, the responsibility is ours, we need to read as much as we can about the candidates and then see if their lives match what the Word of God expects from each of us and then pray.

As we look at the list of characteristics from our scripture reading for today, we need to make a checklist for the candidates. Let us also make an inward checklist for ourselves as well. Do we measure up just as we would expect the candidates to? Some might say, *no one can measure up* and close the book on the matter. One of my professors in college showed us a principle throughout the scriptures: *As goes the leadership, so go the people*.

Since then, I have seen this principle over and over. Whether it is the leader of a country, the leader of a church or the leader of a family, in almost every situation, however the leader rules, the people follow that example. Actually, there are times that I am amazed at how true this principle is and ask myself why I never saw it before? Further, I ask myself if most of the American people can see it.

Throughout scripture God calls us His sheep or compares us to sheep. In this principle given to me by a Godly man, I can see that we truly are sheep that need a Godly shepherd. Not just for the church and family but for the nation.

The power of the position is luring and we need to pray for the person in office. Power and conceit go hand in hand, that lead to sinful patterns. Instead we need to pray that our elected officials remain humble and see their job as a servant leader. The people we vote for should be living a higher standard…the standard that God has put before each of us. It is the standard that we should be striving to meet as well.

Journaling: Write out the above principle and then look to your family. Is the leadership striving to be of good moral character? How about the church you attend? Finally, how about the leadership of your county, state, and nation? What can you do to bring about Godly leadership?

Prayer: Father God, thank you for allowing me to be living in this country. I have a responsibility to pray for the leadership of my country. Please Lord, I ask that You remind me daily to do this. Also Lord, I ask that You fill me with Godly character, for I am a leader to someone else. In Jesus Name…Amen

Personal Challenges:

Day 33

God's Reflection

Reflect: mirror, reveal, expose, ponder

Scripture reading: 2 Samuel 22:26-33

The word "reflect" has many meanings all showing action or state of being.

The scripture reading in some way, seems to suggest that God reflects us but perhaps that is just how we see Him. Let's look at the following illustration.

On a regular basis, a man told his wife how negative she was. Before she had married him, people told her how much she encouraged them, how positive she was, and how she had helped them just by listening. So, how could this husband not see and experience the great qualities that others saw and experienced in his wife? Was she a different person around him? Is she now looking for the negative in people, not finding any good thing?

Amazingly, I have asked God this question for a very long time when He gave me the Scripture in 2 Samuel 22: 26-27 because I believe it is showing us that we reflect those we come into contact with. So, when we are married, we often reflect our partner. If he has integrity, she will reflect integrity; if he is negative, she very well could reflect negativity. May we use Jesus as our example of a servant leader.

It takes a mature Christian to be around someone who does not have Godly characteristics to remain strong in character and, most importantly, to reflect Jesus instead of the spouse. It takes a lot of prayer and searching of your heart to realize that you are reflecting the sinfulness of someone close to you rather than Christ. Personally, I have struggled with this and constantly need Him to guide me, not follow those around me.

The importance of reading God's Word daily is for us to know His character and reflect Him...our Lord, Master, King, Father, Husband, and Brother. What we see in Him should be revealed in us. We make choices as to whom we will serve, whom we will follow, and whom we will reflect.

I know this with my head but still struggle to live out those words day by day. But God is faithful in helping us walk this road. I hope that you are encouraged today to be a reflection of our Lord, for I see Jesus in you.

Journaling: Are you listening to Him this day? Are you reading the Bible to find out how to walk this road? Are you reflecting the One Who longs for you?

Prayer: Heavenly Father, help me to reflect Your image throughout each day. And at those times when I fall short, forgive me and remind me that You give second chances. A chance to ponder Your ways and then do them. In Jesus Name...Amen

Personal Challenges:

Day 34
His Words, Our Words

Words: language, expressions, terminology

Scripture reading: Psalm 119:89, 105; Matthew 22:38; Matthew 12:34b-37

God's Word can bring healing to our weary soul. His Word is our guide in good times and bad times. His Word is as soothing as ointment or it can pierce our heart and bring us to repentance. Pity the person who is not brought to repentance by God's Word.

Just as we see in God's Word, His mighty judgment is on those who will not listen. Even today please know that without repentance, we will experience His judgment. For not only is God a God of love but also a God of justice. He holds the perfect balance, bringing people into our lives to encourage us or bringing people into our lives to show us how badly we need to repent. He is patient. I am thankful for His patience!! But please understand that without repentance we will suffer the consequences of our words and behavior. It is a sure thing, no excuses accepted when we stand before our Lord!

His Word stands firm. His Word reveals how we can live our lives pleasing to Him. We must read the Bible daily in order to let the Holy Spirit quicken our spirit. We must be open to what He is teaching us. We must be obedient to His Word. If His Word does not bring conviction into our hearts and lives, perhaps we need to examine ourselves more closely. Repentance is not a one-time affair but an ongoing, daily purging of one's self. What He says in the Old Testament and what He says in the New Testament are trustworthy.

Today's scripture reading reminds us that our actions and what we say has a deeper root, for it comes from the depths of the heart. When I realized this truth, I decided it was time for me to do a heart checkup, not once but daily.

I speak to myself most of all as a reminder that we must be careful with our words. Having the gift of exhortation is no excuse of speaking rudely to another person or saying words that can cause pain, for God calls us to love others in every way. But what of the person who goes to another in love and that person rejects them? Is it not only the bearer of the words but also the listener who has a responsibility? Is the person really "tearing you apart" or is that person showing God's love in trying to bring you to repentance? We can fool ourselves into thinking that our actions and word are OK but do they measure up to the only Book that matters?

Look at many Old Testament prophets who declared God's Word to a people who would not listen, much less repent. God has a purpose for the entire Bible and we must understand that we are not any different than the Israelites. We lift our hands in holy worship to Him and then we do what is right in our own eyes.

Journaling: Is there anything that hit home with you concerning this day's devotion? Does your heart need a surgical cleaning?

Prayer: Lord, let me start each new day in prayer and repentance before a just and loving God. May I remember that You bring people into my life to purify me. My words need polished and cleaning daily. In Jesus Name…Amen

Personal Challenges:

Day 35

Unity

Unite: fuse together, merge, blend, to combine

Scripture reading: Genesis 45:3-5; Psalm 133:1

As we learned earlier, Joseph had prepared times of testing for his brothers to see if they were straightforward, trustworthy and showed integrity. When he revealed himself to them his brothers didn't know what to say but they knew what they had done to him and were afraid! Can you imagine what they were feeling? The thoughts that ran through their heads? Those images of what they had done to their brother so many years ago were still very real in their minds. But Joseph did not have plans of retaliation.

Joseph learned along the way, that God had actually been the One who sent him to Egypt. God had allowed Joseph to experience much of the cruel treatment but Joseph never grew bitter or hateful. He was teachable! When he tells his brothers that he is Joseph, he has the understanding that God used the past twenty-two years to mold him into a leader that would save his people from certain death. Joseph's heart had gone through the fiery furnace of cleansing so he would be ready for God's purpose.

Joseph says, "Come close to me." He longed for unity with his brothers and his father. He longed for them to be in one accord. This is truly God at work as Joseph reunites with his cruel, dysfunctional family. With his brothers of all people!

Psalm 133:1 reminds us how God feels when we live in unity with one another. <u>Bible Pathway Ministries</u> devotional puts it this way, "It is like many musicians in a great orchestra playing in harmony. There may be a great diversity of instruments, yet there is perfect unity. The word pleasant denotes delightful and lovely. It should be an attitude manifestation towards others." (Bible Pathway, July 08, Vol 35, Num 7, p37)

When brother and sister live together in unity, it delights the Lord. When husband and wife live together in unity, it delights the Lord. When employers and employees live in unity, it delights the Lord. When Christians of all denominations live in unity, it delights the Lord.

As we submit to the Lord, reading His Word daily, taking the principles He is teaching us and applying them to our lives, we will be tested. Maybe not the same as Joseph but there will be times that we may feel much like Joseph did as he was mistreated and sold to the merchants or accused of adultery and sent to jail.

I don't know about you, but I struggle when I am in the middle of a time of testing. I struggle with thoughts of being alone and thinking that no one cares. I pull back from contact with everyone because I am afraid of being rejected. Yes, I do have the Lord in my life and He has sustained me. But He wants more! He wants us to join in unity through those tough times. He wants us to experience the encouragement from others.

Journaling: Are you as teachable as Joseph? Are you able to delight in the Lord through the miseries of life? Make yourself available to at least one hurting person.

Prayer: Dear Jesus, help me to live in unity with those around me, to be willing to come alongside them in love. I thank you for the illustration of Joseph to teach me these valuable lessons. In Jesus Name…Amen

Personal Challenges:

Day 36

Value What is Important

Value: worth, importance, esteem, cherish

Scripture reading: Hebrews 10:24-25; 1 Corinthians 12:12-26

When my late husband retired from the Army, the 89th ARCOM gave a luncheon in which they paid tribute to the many years of dedicated service Jack had given to our country.

I listened with pride at the accomplishments that my husband had done. His fellow workers valued him so much and admired him for serving our country for 40 years. But I was also thinking about how most stay at home moms are just as dedicated to their families and accomplish much more in regard to training the young lives they hold in their hands and yet, no such tribute will ever be heard. Many of us felt God's calling to not work outside the home while our children were growing up, oftentimes giving up financial gain and sometimes going against the grain of modern society.

Shortly after that retirement luncheon, Jack went to Fort Riley, KS for his final paperwork to get out of the Army only to be stopped in his tracks at the hospital because of a questionable chest x-ray. Through much red tape, we found out about ten days later that Jack had inoperable, terminal cancer. They gave him 6 to 18 months to live.

Jack chose not to have any radiation treatment and lived a quality life for 22 months and then, on March 4, 1993, he marched forth into heaven to be with Jesus. Always the military man! It is times like this that we need one another.

Those dear friends and my wonderful pastor, John Green, were there for Jack and I. I will always be grateful to our friend, Doug, who would show up with donut holes for Jack and sit with Jack listening to military tales. And after Jack's passing, these same people continued to be there for me.

We each have a special gift that God wants us to use, to bring glory to Him and to show the outside world that we, as followers of Christ, are different. Remember, sometimes the best gift you can give another person is your time and yourself.

Oh, and the beauty of living the Christian life is that some are there for you years later. Doug and his wife, Sandy, are faithful in sending me an encouraging email each March 4th. I'm sure they have no idea what that email means to me but it is precious and I am thankful. They still remember!

Journaling: Are you a part of a church body and are you actively serving in some capacity? Are you ready to see what God has planned for your life?

Prayer: Thank you Lord for loving me so much as seeing that I have value and can be used. Lord, guide me and teach me along this learning path to give of myself and to remember that it is You that I am truly serving. In Jesus Name…Amen

Personal Challenges:

Day 37

Take and Give

Take: to yield, to secure, to grasp

Give: to commit, to bestow, to present, to impart

Scripture reading: Ephesians 2:4-5; James 2:17;

God has offered us a gift. It is up to us whether we take the gift or leave it sitting at the door of our heart. God loves us so much that He is holding out to you the gift of salvation. What a magnificent choice we have! We can continue living in the sin of this world, serving Satan, who wants us to be self-centered and disobedient or we can serve the living God of the universe. This choice seems like a no-brainer for those who have been in Christ most of their lives. But what about the rest of us?

What a step of faith when we go before the Almighty God and admit that we are sinners and make a conscience decision to want to have Jesus as a part of our life. Is that all there is to the Christian life? Believing that Jesus is the Son of God and continuing to live life as before? In this life-changing step of faith, we will never be the same again. We may even try to go back to our former way of life but there is one difference: we now have Jesus residing in our hearts!

What does it mean to have Jesus as an occupant of our very being? It means that He is a part of our daily lives, and that we look to Him for guidance. He is urging us (through the Holy Spirit) towards a slow but sure change to become more like Him. He accepts you just as you are and where you are but by no means does He want us to stay where we met him. What would a marriage be like if the husband and wife stayed the same throughout their marriage as they were in those first days of their married life? How would a friendship ever flourish if both people never revealed their heart to the other?

We learn how to become more Christ-like through reading the Bible. Not once a week, not once in a while but daily. Get a version of the Bible that you can understand and start reading. This will help you get excited at what God is revealing to you! Then you will find the reason you are His. He gave you the most precious gift of all (salvation) and now you are to give your time, knowledge and finances to Him.

We are nothing without Him! But with Him anything is possible for us to serve. We see example after example throughout the Scriptures of faith being accompanied by action. As we read the Bible daily, we see faith in action and strive to grasp the principles as to how we can put our faith into action.

If you have taken that wonderful gift of Jesus into your heart and soul, why not take the next step and start giving of yourself? There are all sorts of needs of opportunities within the body of Christ, just ask "what can I do?"

Journaling: Have you taken that step of faith and asked Jesus into your life? Find a church and talk to someone in leadership. Now that you've taken that first step, find out how you can give back.

Prayer: Precious Heavenly Father, I am so thankful for the sacrifice that Jesus made for me! Help me Lord to find that opening where I can serve. In Jesus Name…Amen

Personal Challenges:

Day 38

Division

Divide: split, segregate, gulf, rift

Scripture reading: Genesis 11

Not too long ago, I was working as a substitute teacher in a local high school. Many of the students spoke Spanish and, like many students who have a substitute teacher, occasionally insisted on talking only this time it was in Spanish. I felt more frustrated because I could not understand them. Several times, I asked them to speak English, but to no avail. That is one of their ways of messing with a guest teacher and I'm sure their regular teacher as well.

That incident stayed in my head for days. I prayed about it. What could I have done differently? Then out of the blue, God reminded me of a time in Scripture when there was a language problem.

We must go back to Genesis to learn this lesson. The first king of Babylon was Nimrod, whose grandfather was Noah but his father was a bit of a renegade. In fact, Nimrod's name means "the rebel" and a rebel he was. At that point, Gen 11:1 tells us that "the whole world had one language and a common speech." Communication is so much easier when we all speak the same language! I think that the generations before us, here in the United States, recognized what God's Word was saying. Thus, when people came here from other countries, they wanted to learn to speak English.

The people of Babylon showed a principle in scripture that is true today as well as back then. That principle is the same as I talked about earlier: as goes the leadership, so go the people. We can see this principle from families to nations. So now let's look at Babylon once more. This city was ruled by a rebel from a family line of two generations of dissatisfied men. You would think that would not be the case since they were saved from the flood, but there is at least one in every family, isn't there?

Genesis 11 goes on to tell a story of how this group of people was not happy with the way things were. They desired power and thought if they built a tower that reached to heaven, they would make a name for themselves. That tower would be the focal point of the city. They had taken their focus off the Lord and desired it for themselves. Instead of looking to God, they decided to do things their way, their self worth was connected to what they had built.

God finally said enough is enough! These people had turned away from Him so He confused their language and scattered them. This was done for their own good! Therefore, I now have the answer to my pondering.

When a nation turns away from God, when a people is more interested in self esteem/worth, when leaders hold themselves up and put the people down, when laws are made that are directly against the Bible, then God must act. We have allowed prayer to be taken out of the school, detestable practices are now considered as acceptable, so, we no longer serve the Creator of the

Universe and in return, He is allowing our language to be confused and disunity is becoming more prevalent. Judgment is certain, some judgment will happen today and some will experience judgment throughout eternity. God is trying to wake us up...are we listening?

But I know with my whole heart that God is faithful to His own. He will care for us but expects us to do our part to bring others to Him.

Journaling: Is there someone you know that needs a little love today? How about that single mother, that lonely senior citizen or that family next door who just lost their job?

Prayer: Dear Lord, help me not be divisive in my daily walk with You. I give You my hand, my feet, my all to serve You more fully. In Jesus Name...Amen

Personal Challenges:

Day 39

Where Do We Turn?

Turn: go, try, aim

Scripture reading: 2 Chronicles 16:9a; Ephesians 2:10

When our whole world comes crashing down around us, where do we turn? For some of us the feeling of loss can come in the form of health problems, or loss through divorce or death, or a loss dealing with difficult people. This list could go on and on but you get the idea, don't you?

I recently read 2 Chronicles 16:9 and was reminded of our Lord's great love for us. Several words stand out for me and are such an encouragement. Our Lord will strengthen us <u>when</u> our hearts are fully committed to <u>Him</u>. Fully committed to <u>Him</u>! Now that is exciting news!

Are you fully committed to Him? When our world is topsy-turvy, He is waiting for us to call on Him. When our lives are dull, He is waiting for us to reach out to Him. In every stage we find ourselves, we can call on our Lord for assistance. Whether we are hurting or content, that is the exact time to reach out to the Lord.

Dependence on our Father, Lord, Master, King and Husband is not optional. We should have a deep desire to be relational with Him. We are reminded in our scripture reading that God is preparing us so that we may do what He intended. We can see many examples in our lives. When we love someone, we want to give ourselves to that person. We are not required to serve but we <u>desire</u> to serve. Indeed, we demonstrate our love by our actions. Otherwise, how does anyone around us know that we care?

The exciting thing is that He provided a manual so we will know what He expects out of us! Do you have a version of the Bible that you can understand and start reading? Are you ready for one of the most important decision of your life? If you have realized that you are a sinner and want to repent and ask Jesus into your life, take the time right now to talk to Him.

Journaling: This is an important day, a day when you are ready to change your life. Write out some of the sins you can think of, whether small or big, it is good to confess them. After you've prayed the prayer below, seek out a Bible believing church, or a dear Christian friend and tell them what you have done. Get involved in a Bible study. And most importantly, don't forget to read God's Word daily and ask Him to show you what He wants you to learn that day.

Prayer: Heavenly Father, I realize I am a sinful creature and need a Savior. Please forgive my sins and come reside in my heart. From this day forward, I want to live for You. In Jesus Name...Amen

Personal Challenges:

Day 40

Safe in His Arms

Safe: secure, protected, reliable

Scripture reading: Isaiah 54: 4-7

When my military husband marched forth into the loving arms of Jesus, he no longer experienced the pain of cancer. He is healed in the truest sense. Those last 22 months of his life, we lived in the reality of his coming death. We cried, laughed and mourned together as he shared his wisdom with me and I shared my fears with him.

So, when he died, I was ready, right? It is amazing how we can go through life in a numb state and no one seems to recognize that we are hurting. After two weeks, most people stopped talking about Jack. I wanted to continue talking about him but it made most people uncomfortable.

I wish I had listened to Jack's wisdom more and not felt so sorry for myself. Although I have read my Bible almost every day for many years, I did not comprehend for a long time that I have been in the loving arms of Jesus as well. And, even though I have made poor decisions along the way, I am only beginning to realize just why the Lord has allowed me to walk this path. (I may never fully understand until I see Him face to face.)

Along the way, He has protected me from very

dangerous situations. Along the way, He has guided me through college as an adult student. Along the way, He has provided a career beyond motherhood and being a wife, both of which I cherished. Along the way, He has allowed me to experience pain and suffering both emotionally and physically to help me to fall into His loving arms on a regular basis. And along the way, He has loved me when I did not feel anyone else cared.

Although I have read through the Bible numerous times, I am now learning a new appreciation of the life of Abraham and how God worked in His life. He made some bad decisions, lied a time or two, and was no doubt mistreated at some time; he experienced suffering, and he questioned God's promise, but more importantly, Abraham also trusted God as he made his way through life. He learned to trust God more and more with each experience and failure on his part. He also learned to obey. As he obeyed, his faith was strengthened. What a wonderful story of how Abraham was safe in God's loving arms.

Yes, we have God's Word to rely on as we struggle along life's journey. Our Lord cares so much for us that He has given us the Bible so we can see we are not the only ones who make mistakes or put forth great effort just to get through the day. As we learn to obey, we gain more faith and hold on tight to those safe and loving arms.

I am not there yet, but I am learning to rely on Him more and more each day. I still need to be reminded often of His great love for me, and yet I have truly experience His protection in a new way. Hopefully, this will urge you to reach out. Grab your Bible, get on your knees and fall into His arms. Obey even when you do not understand what He's asking you to do.

Even though I know I am here to serve Him for now, I still long for the day when "He will wipe every tear from their [my] eyes. There will be no more death or mourning or crying or pain, for the old order of things has passed away." (Rev 21:4) And I rejoice with you to be held safely in His loving arms.

Journaling: You have made it...all 40 days! Hopefully life has taken on a new meaning and a new challenge. How are you different today as compared to 40 days ago?

Prayer: Thank you Lord for loving me! Thank you Lord for this new life in Christ for I realize that I have changed and am ready to take Your challenges for my life. Lord, I take your hand, and I am so thankful for those times when I can fall into Your loving arms. In Jesus Name...Amen

Personal Challenges:

Final Words

By no means do I want to make anyone feel guilty or shamed for not reading the Bible daily. Nor am I saying that you must live a debt-free life or any of the other illustrations I have used. That is not my intent in writing this devotional. I have shared some of my struggles just as an illustration of what I've been through, hoping it would be an encouragement to you.

This book would not be what it is without the help of many friends and family who took time to pray for me along the way, to read it and make suggestions for improvement. Many thanks go to Karen Baney and Angie Colacouri, who both took time to edit the first draft of this book and to Deb Hickman, Deb Carden, Sarah Dunn, and Teresa for their time and thoughts. These gals have been an encouragement, a guiding light and a faithful beacon of hope. A special thanks to Joyce for her many prayers and Pat Bee for editing the final draft of this book!

Each person is different. For me, I find that <u>Bible Pathway Ministries </u>daily devotional to be just what I need. That may not be what you need. You will probably try different methods in reading and studying the Bible before you find exactly what works for you. I am not a word by word study person but have many friends who are, that's what works for them. The marvel of it all is when you get together with fellow Christians, you can share with one another what God is showing each one of you and see how He has worked it out. The biggest thanks goes to my Lord and Savior. He called me to write a 40 day devotional and then gave me the words. To God be the glory.

Appendix

Different versions of the Bible:

New Living Version (I read this if I know I am going to be in a stressful situation during the next year...it is easier for me to comprehend)

New International Version (understandable, accepted by many scholars);

New King James (has kept much of the poetic words of the KJV)

Works Cited:

Adams, Jay. The Christian Counselor Manual. Grand Rapids, Michigan: Zondervan, 1973.

Avant, John. Authentic Power. Sisters, Oregon: Multnomah Publishers, Inc., 2006.

Bible Pathway Ministries, PO Box 20123, Murfreesboro, TN 37129-0123; Information available at: www.biblepathway.org

Burkett, Larry. <u>The Coming Economic Earthquake</u>. Chicago, Illinois: Moody Press, 1991.

Thomas, Gary. <u>Sacred Marriage</u>. Grand Rapids, Michigan: Zondervan, 2002.

About Author

Fae Dunn has two children and five wonderful grandchildren as well as a special step daughter, two wonderful (step) grand-daughters and four (step) great-grandchildren. She also has several spiritual children/grandchildren that God blessed her with in her old age (so she tells it). She received her bachelor's degree from Grace University in Omaha, NE in 2002, having a dual major in Management/Organizational Leadership and Biblical Studies. One of her passions is encouraging people to live a debt-free life as she serves at Mission Community Church, which is also a place of refuge for Fae. She moved to Mesa, Arizona in 2010 from Nebraska and works as a substitute teacher, NILD educational therapist and now a writer and inspirational speaker. Fae also enjoys traveling and meeting new people.

You may contact Fae at fdunnbook@gmail.com

Personal Thoughts

Made in the USA
Charleston, SC
02 October 2012